MW00945883

Above the

Fray

A Four-Week Bible Study for Those Special Ladies Married to the Badge

Kristi Neace

Copyright Kristi Neace, 2017
All Rights Reserved
Printed in the United States of America
By: CreateSpace.com

Under International Copyright Law, no part of this publication may be reproduced, stored, or transmitted by any means – electronic, mechanical, photographic (photocopy), recording, or otherwise – without written permission from the author.

International Standard Book Number:

ISBN-13:
978-1544676289

ISBN-10:
154467628X

Unless otherwise noted, all Scripture quotations are taken from the HOLY BIBLE, NEW INTERNATIONAL VERSION ®. Copyright © 1973, 1978, 1984 by International Bible Society. Used by permission of Zondervan. All rights reserved.

To God

This wouldn't have been written without you.

I'd like to say a very special thank you to each of the lovely ladies who had my back editing and critiquing – Loren, Doris, Alicia, and Chris…you guys are awesome!

Also, to the other lovelies who sent in their story or thoughts – Carissa, Alicia, Ruth, and Heidi…you rock!

And, to the many others who prayed and encouraged…there's no greater gift.

Table of Contents

Above the Fray

By Kristi Neace - ©2017

Psalm 18:16-19 The Living Bible (TLB)

[16] He reached down from heaven and took me and drew me out of my great trials. He rescued me from deep waters. [17] He delivered me from my strong enemy, from those who hated me—I who was helpless in their hands.

[18] On the day when I was weakest, they attacked. But the Lord held me steady. [19] He led me to a place of safety, for he delights in me.

What *is* a fray? If you look up the meaning of the word, the definition describes it in the form of a verb - *becoming worn and weakened from constant rubbing, such as in a rope, cord or piece of fabric.* Does that sound familiar? If you love a police officer, then you can probably relate.

Dear sister, if this is the first time we've met, then I want to share with you a little piece of my heart. I've lived this life for over 29 years. I understand where you are coming from, as I have walked many miles in your shoes. But I also want to let you know that this journey *can* become the most rewarding challenge of your adult life! You can make it, and I want to give you some tools to help ease the process.

So…buckle up, hang on and get ready! God has a lot to show us about this awesome gift He has given to us called the *law enforcement legacy.* Hopefully by the end, you will no longer be hanging alone by one frayed thread, but will have both hands tightly woven within the strong palms of your Heavenly Father.

What are you waiting for? Let's get going!

Blessings,

Kristi

Worried? Nah, Just Scared to Death!

Week One – Day 1

> *"What time I am afraid, I will trust in thee."* Psalm 56:3 KJV

You know you're a police wife if...

I'll bet you've read those little ditties on social media which include this phrase, but if not, each one gives a silly situation that only someone married to the law would understand.

One of them goes something like: *You know you're a police wife if your best friend, mom, sister and co-workers continually ask if you worry about your husband.* Duh. We would not be human (or not love our husbands) if there wasn't a moment in time we did not worry.

Let's face it...law enforcement is a dangerous occupation, and we've all read the stories of officers not making it home to their families, or we've watched in horror at news reports of an officer using deadly force amid public outcry.

So how do we keep our worry in check?

How do we keep our sanity and not cave in to our fears when it seems as everything around us is falling apart?

Let's take a look back at some other folks who were struggling with worry and fear. Read the passage then answer the question.

> John 20:19-27 – What did Jesus tell his disciples three times while they were in a locked room, hiding from those who might want to harm them?

> What does this say to us today regarding our present circumstances?

> Acts 1:12-14 – What were the disciples and women doing during this time of persecution and waiting?

> How important is it that we pray when feeling worried or uptight, and why?

Looking back at your questions, the first set of scriptures revolve around the disciples immediately following Christ's betrayal, crucifixion and death.

Jesus had been well-known throughout Jerusalem and the surrounding towns, and was never without his beloved entourage. Just as in law enforcement life, these individuals were living in a glass bubble and everyone knew who they were.

After witnessing such horrific and hurtful acts of violence towards their beloved teacher, the disciples were afraid and hid themselves in a locked room. We can rest assured there were no bumper stickers linking them with being a Christ-follower; no "I'm with Jesus" t-shirts. These men (and women) were scared and fearing for their lives.

Yet, Jesus knew the anguish they were going through. He cared deeply for them just as He cares deeply for you and me today. So much so, that He made it His mission to *personally* comfort and reassure them.

"Peace be with you!"

Those words rolled off His tongue with authority and confidence, yet they were more comforting than a mother's embrace. Jesus was alive and He wanted them to let go of their fears, knowing that He had overcome the worst human fear of all...death.

Can you just imagine? Have you ever been scared and alone, not knowing what to do or where to go, and then, out of nowhere, someone you love deeply comes to your rescue? Ahh...what relief!

> A number of years ago, I had traveled by myself to a conference in Kansas City, Missouri. Now, I'm not one who likes to travel alone, but I was part of a women's ministry team and was speaking at a break-out session. I made the 4-hour trek by myself. Late that evening, after the conference had ended for the night, each of us made our way back to the hotel except for me. It was late and I was tired. A blinding rain was falling which made it harder for me to see. I was in unfamiliar territory and without a GPS. The plan was for me to follow behind a friend of mine; however, in all the confusion, I missed my turn. I was lost, and now found myself on an interstate going towards Wichita, Kansas. To say I freaked puts it mildly. I got off the interstate and entered a...let me see...not so good part of town. Visions of being hacked to pieces and thrown in the river taunted me, and I felt sad that my officer husband would never know what happened. Sigh. I worried. I began tearing up. I prayed. Finally, I stopped and called my man. His calming voice on the other end of the phone soothed my fears. Though my anxiety had pretty much taken over, he gave me enough sense to get back on the interstate and find my way back to where I had started, and eventually to the hotel.

❦ Have you ever had to face a frightening situation, but God somehow reassured you that everything would be okay? Explain here:

In Acts 1, we see the men and women again, huddled together in the upper room. This time, however, instead of imagining them wringing their hands and pacing the floor, they were actively seeking a solution through prayer.

Sweet sister, there are going to be many occasions when fearful and worrisome times come your way. There will be *those* calls when your husband leaves for a hostage situation or a pursuit; when all chaos breaks loose and it seems as if the world is coming for your man...and you, with daggers and torches. Don't be shaken.

Those are the moments when you must spring into action. Prayer is your weapon of victory. Not only will God fill you with His overwhelming peace, but He will give you the level-headedness to make wise decisions, to not overreact, and/or to wait patiently for that "all's clear" call after the fact.

When I was a little girl, my momma always quoted this simple scripture to me, and it has served me well over the years, so I want to share it with you, *What time I am afraid, I will trust in you.* Psalm 56:3.

Join with me as I pray over our officers today, for our peace and assurance to know that *He* has your back.

Dear Father,

Thank You for being a loving God who comforts us and is concerned for our peace of mind. I pray today that You will shelter our officers and keep them hidden away from the enemy who wants to destroy them. I pray that You will help us know that even in the dark times, we can trust You to see us through. Lord, give us clear direction and help us to always find our solace in You.

In Your Son's Holy Name, Amen.

See you tomorrow, friend.

Kristi

The Unwanted Stranger

Week One - Day 2

"Worry does not empty tomorrow of its sorrow, it empties today of its strength." –
Corrie Ten Boom

When you are a cop's wife, there always seems to be this huge elephant in the room. It's not talked about, but it's there all the same.

We tend to move things around it...clean up after it, but still it lingers. What am I talking about? Oh, you know...that unwanted stranger, the "What If?".

So, what does this "What If?" look like? Well let me give you my own personal scenario from past thoughts:

Routine:

Rick leaves for his midnight shift.

Me: Yay! I finally get some free time to myself after the kids go to bed. I may read…take a long refreshing bath, or catch up on my shows!

(After mandatory mom duties, Kristi takes in some of her planned activities then retreats to bed)

Me: Aahhh. This feels good. I can stretch out on the bed and…

(hears a noise in the basement)

Me: What was that? Oh, probably nothing. Just go to sleep.

(Dog next door begins barking viciously)

Me: What is going on?

(Gets up and looks out the window then jumps back in bed)

Me: Go to sleep, Kristi. It's nothing.

(Tosses and turns for an hour or so and double checks to make sure the gun is still under her pillow)

Me: What if something happened to him? What if they come to get me? What would I wear?

(Flips back over)

Me: Would he know that I *do* love him even though I vent my frustrations more than my thoughts of love? Who would I get to come stay with the kids? How would I tell them? If...heaven forbid...something terrible happens, would I stay in this house or sell?

(Kristi finally falls asleep, then awakens to Rick tripping over the extra bed pillows piled up in the floor. Thankfulness settles in and sleep commences. Another night down.)

Okay, so your scenario may look a little different than this, but generally, we wives have all had those "What if" thoughts. So what do we do with those? How do we quiet our mind and allow God to take control of those endless questions and concerns that try and rob us of our sanity?

Read the following passage in Matthew 6:25-34. Underline everything God tells us not to worry about.

Matthew 6:25-34New International Version (NIV)

[25] "Therefore I tell you, do not worry about your life, what you will eat or drink; or about your body, what you will wear. Is not life more than food, and the body more than clothes? [26] Look at the birds of the air; they do not sow or reap or store away in barns, and yet your heavenly Father feeds them. Are you not much more valuable than they? [27] Can any one of you by worrying add a single hour to your life?

[28] "And why do you worry about clothes? See how the flowers of the field grow. They do not labor or spin. [29] Yet I tell you that not even Solomon in all his splendor was dressed like one of these. [30] If that is how God clothes the grass of the field, which is here today and tomorrow is thrown into the fire, will he not much more clothe you—you of little faith? [31] So do not worry, saying, 'What shall we eat?' or 'What shall we drink?' or 'What shall we wear?' [32] For the pagans run after all these things, and your heavenly Father knows that you need them. [33] But seek first his kingdom and his righteousness, and all these things will be given to you as well.

[34] Therefore do not worry about tomorrow, for tomorrow will worry about itself. Each day has enough trouble of its own.

What are some reasons the Father gives us for not worrying?

Here's the thing, friend, if we don't face that elephant head on...if we continue to act like it isn't there, we fool ourselves. God never said that we wouldn't have those "What if's" enter our lives, but He did make sure to tell us how valuable we are to Him, including our husband, family, livelihood, etc. He knows that if our focus is on that huge elephant, then our eyes are not on Him.

Read the following passage in Psalm 25:15-21, and insert the word or words that are missing (I used the NIV version).

"My _____ are ever on the _____, for only he will release my feet from the _____. Turn to me and be gracious to me, for I am _____ and _____. The troubles of my heart have multiplied; free me from my anguish. Look upon my _____ and my _____ and take away all my sins. See how my enemies have increased and how fiercely they hate me! Guard my life and rescue me ; let me not be put to shame, for I take _____ in you. May _____ and _____ protect me, because my _____ is in you."

Okay, do you see it? Do you see through these words written by David that tell you, you are not alone? Many have walked, are walking and will walk the very same path you are on, but here's the beauty of it...God is our hope! David knew it and we can know it too.

Yes, there are bad things happening all around us: Yes, it is increasing. Yes, these things can leave us depleted and fearful. That elephant in the room can suck the life out of us if we let it. Yet, our God is faithful! Our God is our Great Rescuer and can illuminate the darkness. He can set us free from our afflictions and grant us refuge within His great love.

So, the next time you are feeling like the "What ifs" have trampled all over you and it's hard to even breathe, remember to *look up* for our Redeemer draweth nigh!

❧ What is your "What If" story? How have you dealt with the fears and frustrations you have felt in those difficult moments?

Dear Precious Lord,

Thank you for Your assurance that You will be with me no matter what I may have to face. Thank you that You are trustworthy and true and are my shelter in the storms of life. Help me to keep my eyes on You and give You my worries and concerns. In Your Holy name, Amen.

Have a restful, peace-filled sleep friend. God is in control.

Kristi

Week One - Day 3

> Around the year 2009, a friend of ours - a Texas deputy, received a call of a domestic in progress. "John" and another deputy pulled up and began to make their way to the front porch, when all of a sudden, a man flung open the door and began firing on the officers. John's partner immediately succumbed to his wounds and John was badly injured with facial and other type injuries, yet, he managed to crawl up under his patrol car to keep himself hidden and out of the line of fire. Unable to call for help, John was defenseless against this crazed man with a gun. Eventually, in a God-ordained moment, a friend just happened to dial John's cell phone, not realizing the officer was working, or more importantly fighting for his life. John was able to somehow communicate his need for help, and the friend was able to get the information to the command center. Deputies eventually arrived and John's life was spared, but not without leaving lasting post-traumatic stress effects on him and his family.

What do we do when and if the unthinkable happens? How do we respond? In John's case, his physical injuries healed, but the emotional scars were not as easy to erase. The stress on his marriage from the nightmares and the recurring panic attacks eventually won out and John was left alone to battle the demons that continued to taunt him.

How would you and I react to something like this if the shoe were on the other foot, or if this was our spouse? What does God's Word say about our enemy and the power he holds over us?

Look up the following verses and write the word or words that best describe the overall theme.

Example: 1 Peter 3:13-14: *"Who is going to harm you if you are eager to do good? But even if you should suffer for what is right, you are blessed. Do not fear what they fear, do not be frightened."* **Answer:** <u>Do not fear, even in suffering</u>

1 Peter 5:8-10:

Romans 8:34-39:

Sister, we *may* endure some trials. Bad things and bad people *may* come into our life, but even so, understand that you are not alone in those moments. We are not to fear them, but trust God's sovereignty in all of it.

Lamentations 3:37-38 says, *"Who can speak and have it happen if the Lord has not decreed it? Is it not from the mouth of the Most High that both calamities and good things come?"*

- Why do you think the Lord "decrees" or allows bad things to happen to those He loves?

We may never understand this side of Heaven why things happen the way they do. I'm sure Job from the Old Testament had a hard time understanding why everything he owned, his health, and all ten of his children were taken away in one day.

However, what Job could not see is that Satan had been given permission by God to bring turmoil into Job's life to a point, in order to test and prove the genuineness of his faith. Job was to be put through the refiner's fire, and he would come out stronger and more pure than before he went in. Hard lesson, but so effective.

❦ Have you ever been put through a difficult test? Perhaps not directly, but one you've reaped the "benefits" from as it happened to your spouse, a close family member or someone you love? Please describe:

Take a look back at the story of Job by reading Job 13:15 and 23:10-17. What is his overall attitude towards God during this time of difficulty and do you think he recognized it as something much deeper than what he could see/feel?

Thankfully, we have the rest of the story. We can read through the pages of Job and see that indeed, God brought him through and blessed him even more than before! Job was never alone in his suffering. God was there and was using every hardship to draw His servant closer to Him.

David – a man after God's own heart, was another one who faced many trials. Some he brought on himself, but most were allowed in his life to strengthen his character and faith. From running from King Saul who wanted him dead, to hiding from his son, Absalom, who wanted the throne, David struggled with hardship, yet knew from where his help was found.

Read the following verses and circle the words or phrases that describe God's provision and goodness towards those going through tough times.

"O LORD, how many are my foes! How many rise up against me!...But you are a shield around me, O LORD; you bestow glory on me and lift up my head. To the LORD I cry aloud, and he answers me from his holy hill." Psalm 3:1, 3-4

"I will fear no evil, for you are with me; your rod and your staff, they comfort me. You prepare a table before me in the presence of my enemies. You anoint my head with oil; my cup overflows." Psalm 23:4b-5

"To you, O LORD, I lift up my soul; in you I trust, O my God. Do not let me be put to shame, nor let my enemies triumph over me. No one whose hope is in you will ever be put to shame..." Psalm 25:1-3a

"I will be glad and rejoice in your love, for you saw my affliction and knew the anguish of my soul. You have not handed me over to the enemy but have set my feet in a spacious place." Psalm 31:7-8

"The eyes of the LORD are on the righteous and his ears are attentive to their cry..." Psalm 34:15

"The LORD redeems his servants; no one will be condemned who takes refuge in him." Psalm 34:22

These are just a small selection of verses that demonstrate God's love for us. Not only does He comfort and anoint, but He prepares a table fit for a king all while our enemies look on.

God fights for us! All we have to do is exactly what Exodus 14:14 says: *"The LORD will fight for you; you need only to be still."*

Sister, what is it that you are struggling with today? Are you wrestling with fears of a very real and present enemy, or feeling oppressed by the lies of the devil? Do not forget, you are wholly loved by a holy King! He will fight this battle for you; all you have to do is be still and trust Him.

Dear Lord...thank you that we can trust you! You are our rock and our shield. You fight for us when we cannot hold the battle line. I pray that you will strengthen and encourage each precious one who is walking through this study. Give them a peace that passeth all understanding, and help them to know that You are for them; therefore, who can be against them?! In your precious Son's name, Amen.

See you tomorrow, friend!

Kristi

Finding Peace in the Midst of the Storms

Week One - Day 4

> *"I'm not afraid of storms, for I'm learning how to sail my ship."*
> --Louisa May Alcott

This morning, I awoke to news of an officer who had been shot in our area, and was being reported as in critical condition. It's sad to say, but there have been so many of these recently, that though I was saddened to hear, I simply pushed it out of my mind and went on with my morning routine. I ate breakfast, got dressed and went to work. It was only then I found out the officer had succumbed to his wounds. He was thirty-three years old, a husband to a young wife, a dad to a toddler, a man with a heart for others...active in his church...a volunteer at a community center for kids in trouble.

As the facts came in, I began to crumble. Why?! Why another, Lord? The pain welled up inside. The "What ifs" tormented me, but more importantly the defiant anger toward this skewed attitude that a "good cop is a dead one."

Friend, this is reality. I wish it weren't. I wish we could somehow go back to Mayberry where bullets were optional and the biggest fear was being late for dinner. Yet, here we are in the 21st Century where violence has become all too personal.

If you are on social media police spouse sites, chances are good that one of your "friends" will experience some type of devastating news. It may not be a shooting, but it could be a diagnosis of PTSD (Post Traumatic Stress Disorder), a demand for divorce, the loss of a job, charges being filed against their spouse for taking action, or a whole host of other scenarios.

So, what's our course of action? How do we face these fears head on and continue putting up that brave front? And, does it really have to be a front? Can we find total peace in the midst of chaos? Let's take a look!

*Turn with me to the book of Acts, starting in Chapter 27, verse 13.

In this passage, we see Paul, a prisoner, on a ship headed to Rome. We also read that there was a huge storm brewing on the open sea threatening to destroy all within its reach.

What was Paul's advice to the men of the ship? (verse 22)

What do you think he meant by that? (Read down through verse 25)

Now, look over at verses 33-36. What did Paul urge them to do in the midst of their storm and in preparation for their deliverance?

Okay, so you are probably thinking: "How does this tie into what I experience as a police spouse?" Let me explain:

Our fears can so paralyze us that we can become a prisoner to them just as Paul was a literal prisoner to his earthly chains. You know, the enemy has a way of binding up our mind and heart, creating such strong emotions that we can do nothing but sit and stew and worry over things completely out of our control.

Yet, like Paul, Jesus tells us throughout His Word, that we are to take courage…to *be encouraged*…to not fear. Why? Because He knows the plans for us on the other side of that storm. We may not always be able to see what the outcome is going to be, but He knows.

As we jumped on down to the latter verses, we see that Paul had such confidence in His God, that he encouraged the sailors to take bread and eat, an every day, ordinary task in the middle of the storm. Do you and I still have the peace of mind to forge ahead…to complete the ordinary tasks God has given us to do, even while the winds are raging, or, do we crumble: Not able to think straight, sleep, eat or function half-way normally?

How could Paul be so chilled out in a serious situation like this? What do you think gave Paul this peace-filled mindset when all chaos had broken loose?

Sweet friend, it's not easy, but we are given a choice. We can either allow our circumstances to overwhelm us, or we can weather the storm with God as our anchor of peace. I don't know about you, but I choose the anchor!

- ❧ **Describe a time when you were really struggling with finding peace. What steps did you take to get through?**

Turn with me to John 14:27. Jesus and His disciples are gathered in the upper room having those final intimate moments of fellowship with one another before He would be arrested and killed. Let's read His words to them, but insert your name at the very beginning of the verse.

<u>(Name)</u> – *"Peace I leave with you; my peace I give you. I do not give to you as the world gives. Do not let your hearts be troubled and do not be afraid."*

How does that make you feel?

Do these words bring you any sense of comfort?

What do you think He meant by saying, "I do not give to you as the world gives"?

Listen, friend, this world is going to try and give you solutions on how to deal with the stresses of this crazy life. I see it every single day on social media and I'm sure you do as well.

Many will tell you that your spouse simply needs to be more understanding of your worry, others will invite you into their web of unhealthy attitudes and actions.

Simply put, the world cannot give you the peace that God can. We can search the world over, try many different tricks or tips, experiment with a whole host of remedies, but nothing will completely satisfy and comfort us.

I want to end this day's lesson with you writing God a letter. I want you to tell Him everything that is on your heart – those things weighing you down causing you to feel shaken and on edge. When you've written your thoughts, close your eyes and sit very still. Ask Him to simply overwhelm you with His presence. I promise you, sweet one, He won't leave you hanging. His peace will surround and strengthen you. He loves you so!

Dear Jesus…

Shalom (peace),

Kristi

Clinging to the Rock that is Higher than I

Week One - Day 5

From the ends of the earth I call to you, I call as my heart grows faint; lead me to the rock that is higher than I. - Psalm 61:2

I just returned home from the young officer's funeral…the one I mentioned in the Day 4 lesson. While there, I felt my heart racing just a bit; my palms a little sweatier than normal.

You see, just this past Monday in the wee hours of the morning, our son who is an officer in a nearby town, pulled over a suspicious vehicle. The woman jumped out of the truck and proceeded to the front, out of sight of my son. He exited his patrol car and gave her orders to get back in the truck. She said that she didn't have to listen. He ordered her to re-enter her truck. As he tried to handcuff her, she turned on him, repeatedly kicking and hitting him. As things escalated, she called to her man who exited the truck and jumped on our son's back grabbing for his service weapon. Thankfully it was still safely latched in its holster. God had been waking me up repeatedly throughout that night and impressing upon me to pray. He gave our son the strength to overtake both the man and woman until help could arrive.

Sweet friend, there will be times when we feel a little bit knocked kneed, as if the rug has been pulled out from under us. There will be days that even though we know in our hearts that God is good, things won't seem so good at that moment.

So what do we do? How do we handle those instances when we cannot find the strength to continue? I tell you what we do. We run to the Rock who is higher than we are. That's what I've had to do this week. That's what I will continue to do until the dust settles on this one and the next crisis comes into play.

Has God ever awakened you at night to pray for your spouse or someone you love? How did that scenario play out?

Turn with me to Genesis 32:22-32, read it then ask yourself the following questions:

1. **What is the scene here? Who was the man and why was he alone?**

2. What happened to the man while wrestling with the "stranger"?

3. What was the blessing that was given to him by the "stranger"?

Okay, so this is a great story! For a little background, Jacob was a twin, the son of Isaac and Rebecca, grandson of Abraham. Jacob had cheated his brother Esau out of his birthright and blessing, by disguising himself as his brother, and fooling his elderly blind father. Sounds like a bad soap-opera, doesn't it?

Jacob had been on the run from his brother and had worked a total of 14 years for his two wives, Rachel and Leah, and now was returning home to face his brother, not knowing what the outcome would be.

Jacob had sent his wives, children and possessions ahead of himself, and had settled down for the night alone. That is, until God showed up in a huge way! He was "accosted" by an Angel of the Lord (God in human form), and they wrestled to and fro all night long. You can imagine how exhausting an exchange of that magnitude would have been, but also how frightening not understanding *Who* it was that he was wrestling.

At daybreak, the Lord touched his hip, causing great pain, yet Jacob held on and would not let go until the Lord blessed him. Because of that situation, God changed Jacob's name to "Israel," which held great significance for generations to come.

So again, how does this relate to our wrestling in prayer for ourselves or our LEOs?

There will be times when this life becomes overwhelming. Trials will come at us and sleep will evade. However, it is in those times we need to "wrestle" with God. He is the only One strong enough…powerful enough to adequately handle and provide the answers we seek.

Like Jacob, there will be moments when our wrestling seems to go on without end. You and I might even experience pain in the process – a wounding of our heart and soul. Yet, if we stay the course…if we continue the match, God will honor our persistence and in many instances give us a new perspective, attitude, or strength.

❀ **What would you say are some of the most taxing things you wrestle with? Explain.**

Let's take a bit of a detour now and learn about some of the characteristics of God that help us in our hour of need. ***Match the verses on the left with the description on the right.**

Verse	Description
Psalm 46:1	Source of wisdom
2 Corinthians 1:3-5	Healer
Psalm 28:7	Protector
Psalm 91:1-2	Refuge & strength/help in trouble
James 1:5	Comfort in affliction
Psalm 103:3	Strength/shield

See, friend, God is so many things for us…more than anyone else can be. He is greater than any human and truer than any friend. He will be there for and provide exactly what you and I need when we need it, but the key is in the asking.

This week, if you find yourself in a place that is uncomfortable and simply out of control, run to the Rock - our loving Heavenly Father, and allow Him to wrestle it out with you. You are sure to be blessed!

Dear Father,

I pray that You shelter us with Your heavenly arms today. Help us know that You are trustworthy and we can come to You…should come to You, when everything seems to be falling around us. You alone are worthy. You alone can save. We love and trust You today. Amen.

Many blessings over the coming days. You are loved!

Kristi

A Note From a Police Wife…

Some days I really struggle with daily life. I feel like I am making wrong choices, or disappointing someone. Some days I struggle just fitting in. God has placed me in a unique place in my life. I am a Christian, a wife of a law enforcement officer, a mother of three teenage boys, a homemaker, and some days feel like Wonder Woman. I also believe I need more hours in the day! So what do I do to get through each day?

I pray, read the Bible, or I recite two very important verses in my life. Proverbs 3:5-6 *"Trust in the Lord with all your heart, and do not lean on your own understanding. In all your ways acknowledge him, and he will make straight your paths."* And Psalm 32:8 *"I will instruct you and teach you in the way you should go; I will counsel you with my eye upon you."* Recently I've found this comforting. I try and pray every day that God's will be done with my day, and that He will lead me in His way. These verses teach me that God's word is the truth. He will lead me by His word. He guides me by His will. God's way is true and perfect.

 When I recite these verses I know God has a plan for my family and me. I'll admit some days are rougher than others. I often feel alone due to my husband's shift work, and I also struggle with Rheumatoid Arthritis which can take its toll on my stamina, therefore, I try to make the house as peaceful and relaxing as I can.

Times can be tough in the world we live in. You and I need to remember we always have God in our corner. The life behind the badge can be rough on anyone. I have been an LEOW for 19 years, and after many solo appearances for holidays, sports or school events, and milestones, I realize that the glue which holds the family together truly is the wife. It took me many years, lots of tears and sleepless nights till I was able to really understand my husband's job and the life that goes with it.

Remember this, you are not alone. You always have God, your spouse and hopefully some understanding and supportive family and friends. You and I need to keep praying and focusing on these verses, and try to make the best of everyday for we never know when they'll come to an end. Take these verses as an encouragement for your life. God knows your path, and He will guide you…just wait on Him. You never know but you may be a Wonder Woman too!

Carissa Cassel

Home Alone…Again!

Week 2 – Day 1

> *The best remedy for those who are afraid, lonely or unhappy is to go outside,*
> *somewhere where they can be quiet, alone with the heavens, nature and God.*
> *Because only then does one feel that all is as it should be.*
> *- Anne Frank*

Loneliness. It can be one of the hardest adjustments to law enforcement life.

I remember back to when my husband and I were dating, and then our first year or so together, we were inseparable. After academy, however, when the swing shifts began taking over our lives, the overtime hours and unexpected call-ins, loneliness within me set in and began to breed resentment.

I hear many police wives comment about how lonely they get. I think that's why social media has become such a popular thing. It's that imaginary outlet where we have "friends" without strings - connections for those alone times. In some respects it is a good thing, but more often than not, it can become a deterrent keeping us from finding true inner peace and contentment through the presence of a holy God.

Have you ever had those moments when you were feeling lonely and perhaps resentful towards your spouse because of the long hours away? Describe how you handled those feelings and what you did to occupy yourself.

Let's take a look at some verses that deal with loneliness. Underline the word or phrase which describes what the Lord will do for us.

"So do not fear, for I am with you; do not be dismayed, for I am your God. I will strengthen you and help you; I will uphold you with my righteous right hand." Isaiah 41:10

"…for the LORD your God goes with you; he will never leave you nor forsake you." Deuteronomy 31:6

"If the Lord had not been my help, my soul would soon have lived in the land of silence." Psalm 94:17 ESV

"He will call on me, and I will answer him; I will be with him in trouble, I will deliver him and honor him." Psalm 91:15

"At my first defense, no one came to my support, but everyone deserted me. May it not be held against them. But the Lord stood at my side and gave me strength..." 2 Timothy 4:16&17a

"A father to the fatherless, a defender of widows, is God in his holy dwelling. God sets the lonely in families, he leads out the prisoners with singing; but the rebellious live in a sun-scorched land." Psalm 68:5-6

Looking at these verses, we see that if we allow Him, God will strengthen and uphold us. He truly is One we can count on; He will never leave us nor forsake us. He is our help and our deliverer. He gives us honor, will stand at our side, and sets us in families. Did you catch all that?!

The bottom line is when you and I are feeling lonely and abandoned, God is there! We simply have to learn to take those feelings and give them to Him.

So how do we do that? How do we go from feeling completely left out, to walking with our head held high and a spirit of peace over every thought? Well, it takes a little work and practice, but can be done. Take a look below.

Lonely Without Seeking God's Help

- Feels sorry for self
- Begins to justify anger
- Plays the blame game
- Entertains resentment
- Looks for other things/people to fill void

Lonely, But Seeking God's Help

- Learns to take eyes off self and focus on others
- Releases anger to God
- Seeks to understand, not blame
- Does not give resentment a foothold
- Allows God to fill the void

I know you are probably thinking, "Well, that is easier said than done", and you're right! I've been there many times. The key to surviving this crazy lifestyle is a relationship with the Lord. Does that mean we will never again feel alone or angry or taken advantage of? No.

What it does mean is that He can take those feelings of resentment and hurt, and help us refocus. Instead of finding fault with our husbands, we can seek ways to help them. In place of that bitterness, we can take satisfaction in the fact that 1.) Our husbands are holding down a job, 2.) They have a job to hold down, and 3.) Our husbands and God have confidence in our abilities to juggle the responsibilities we have in their absence.

When we are daily seeking after God, He begins to fill us with a peace that "passes all understanding". No longer do we spend our time chasing after the wind, but instead chase hard after Him. In return, He fills our tank, gives us a firm footing, strengthens us to carry out our tasks, etc. And here's the kicker…when we are feeling full and satisfied and complete and purposeful, it is likely our marriage will be full and satisfied and complete and purposeful. C'mon, give it a try! Listen, I only know this because I've lived it. Wink.

Tomorrow's lesson we will dig in a little more to the topic of being lonely and feeling like a single parent, but before we go, let's look at one more verse I want you to write down somewhere where you can see it each and every day. This is another oldie but goodie my mom would quote to me, so I'm going to speak it over you….

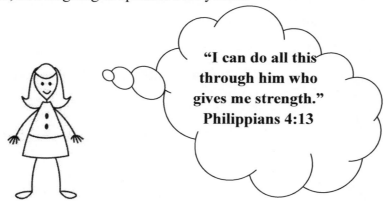

"I can do all this through him who gives me strength."
Philippians 4:13

✿ **What steps are you going to take today to ensure that you keep your loneliness in check?**

You can do it, momma! See you tomorrow.

Kristi

The Single Parent Syndrome: How to Cope as a Single in a Two-Parent Home

Week 2 - Day 2

Welcome back! Yesterday we talked a little bit about the loneliness we can experience as the wife of an officer.

Today we are going to cover the feelings of being a single parent in a two-person home. You know, single parenting is hard, but it has even more of a sting when there are actually two parents in the home – one of which happens to be an LEO.

> Thinking back, I can recall one particularly stressful evening when one of our children decided to display his pre-teen independence. Of course, dad was at work and I was extremely tired and not in any mood to corral this young buck. So, in my frustration I found myself in the middle of a shouting match resulting in hurt feelings on both ends and an adolescent on the run. After a couple of hours and with dark setting in, I called my husband in an anxious panic. Our son had not returned home and I had no idea where to look. Because Rick was tied up on calls, another officer was sent to scour the countryside looking for our lost little lamb. Eventually, he was found sitting at Wal-Mart a couple miles down the road, stubbornly waiting the situation out.

It's at times like this, that we as wives and mothers, want to pull out our hair. I remember thinking, *why can't I have a husband with a normal 8-5:00 job that is home in the evenings to help me? I didn't sign up to be a single parent!*

So how do we cope with the frustration and the loneliness? We turn to God's Word and eat mounds of chocolate!

Shouldering the responsibility of rearing children, taking care of a household, holding down a job outside of the home, and trying to carve out quality time for you and your husband, not to mention yourself, can be daunting. Many emotions can arise as you experience the highs and lows, the aggravations and the headaches. Let's look at some of these emotions and what the Bible has to say:

Anger

What characteristics are given to God with regard to *His* anger? (Exodus 34:6, Numbers 14:18, Nehemiah 9:17, Psalms 86:15, Psalm 103:8, Jonah 4:2)

I guess you saw the pattern here. So, how should we strive to respond when our frustrations have gotten the best of us?

Look at Proverbs 29:11 – What does the Bible call one who spouts off in anger?

What is the challenge to each of us in Ephesians 4:26-27?

What do you think it means when it says, "and do not give the devil a foothold"?

These scriptures are definitely a challenge to us all, but wait...there is more! ☺

Resentment/Bitterness

1 Corinthians 13:1-13 – What is a key ingredient to battle resentment and bitterness?

Describe what love is:

Ephesians 4:31-32 – What are we supposed to do with our bitterness (resentment)? And, what does God call us to do instead?

James 5:16 – How are we to stay accountable and on track with our emotions?

Anxiety/Worry

Philippians 4:6-7 – What does God tell us to do when we are anxious?

What happens when we go straight to Him with our worry?

Psalm 55:22 – What is another thing God promises to do for us if we turn to Him?

Jealousy/Envy

James 3:14-16 – What does God say about jealousy/envy in this passage?

What does jealousy and envy lead to (vs. 16)?

What do you think the opposite of jealousy would be?

Philippians 4:11-13 – What was Paul saying about his circumstances?

❦ **What does this passage tell us about being content with our current situation? *If you are in a group study, be ready to share your answer.**

I hope these verses have spoken to your heart. It is not easy being the wife of a law officer, yet God chose you for this special task, as well as did your husband. Stand firm, keep the main thing the main thing (God), and everything else will work itself out.

Blessings to you, my friend.

Kristi

The Invisible Woman

Week 2 - Day 3

> *"So, I'm invisible to you now? That's cool, I've always wanted a superpower."* -
> Lolsotrue:#2329

Have you ever felt invisible? It is a painful place to be, I assure you. I have known invisibility first hand as I've always battled shyness, and then…I married a cop. The invisibility factor did not diminish, but only grew louder.

I don't know if you've ever experienced this feeling. I pray you haven't. I so wish we could sit down over a good meal or an iced coffee and talk about this very real factor. Yet, I guess it will have to suffice to discuss it over the next several pages.

You know, we are never invisible to God. He knows our name and everything about us. The Bible tells us that *He knit us together in our mother's womb* and that *every one of our hairs is numbered.* Yet, even knowing those things, with an occupation like our husband's, we can still sometimes feel the sting of invisibility. Let me explain…

> Tanya had been married to Joe for twelve years. During that time, Joe continued to move up the ladder at work, while Tanya stayed at home and raised their two children. Joe had the shiny badge. He had a name tag. Everyone in their small town knew Joe and loved him. When they would go to social gatherings, Tanya was known as "Joe's wife" or "Brady and Jordan's mom". She had somehow lost her identity and had become somewhat invisible. And not only that, Joe had become so preoccupied with his career, that Tanya became second fiddle. He no longer put forth an effort to make her feel special and important. Tanya's world began to seemingly cave in on her and she felt as if she was simply a nobody. Anyone relate?

I don't know if the above scenario fits you or not, but it sure fit me when our children were small. Though I did work outside of the home for most of their growing up years, there was a time period when we had moved to a new community and I stayed at home.

Quickly, I began to believe I was a nobody, and with that feeling came dissatisfaction and even depression. *I was placing my identity and fulfillment in the hands of my husband…*an extremely dangerous position.

Have you ever felt invisible and if so, what did you do to correct it?

Let's take a look at what God's Word says about who we are. Read the following verses and circle the word or words that best describe how God sees us.

But to all who have received him--those who believe in his name--he has given the right to become God's children. John 1:12

I no longer call you slaves, because the slave does not understand what his master is doing. But I have called you friends, because I have revealed to you everything I heard from my Father. John 15:15

And if children, then heirs (namely, heirs of God and also fellow heirs with Christ)--if indeed we suffer with him so we may also be glorified with him. Romans 8:17

For we are his workmanship, having been created in Christ Jesus for good works that God prepared beforehand so we may do them. Ephesians 2:10

These are just a few of the many verses that God lays out in His Word about our worth. He loves us so much…we were and are so precious to Him, that He sent His Son to die on the cross for us! There is no greater love.

Therefore, when you and I begin to believe in the lies Satan throws our way about being unimportant or invisible, we grieve the heart of God.

Before we go for today, let's take a look at a woman in the New Testament who felt invisible yet Jesus made it a point to stop and encourage her.

Read the story about the Samaritan woman in John 4, and then answer the questions below:

Where did Jesus "happen" to meet this lonely lady?

What did He ask her to do?

What was her response?

How did Jesus approach her sinful lifestyle?

What was her response?

Okay, so to recap a wonderful story that we can all learn something from…

Jewish people had nothing to do with Samaritans for they were considered unclean and were "half-breeds" (Jews intermarried with pagan peoples from other places).

Upstanding Jews would go to great lengths to steer clear of them and their town, by going miles out of their way to avoid making contact. But even in the midst of the "invisibles" there was this woman who would have won the crown for least popular. She had a reputation amongst the locals and resorted to avoiding the taunts and shaming from her fellow countrymen, by drawing water at the hottest part of the day instead of waiting until evening when all the women drew water.

It was there that she met the King of the world - Jesus. He took the time to talk with her. He asked her for a drink, a request so scandalous for a Jewish Rabbi, as He would drink from the same cup she had sipped from.

He laid out her sins, yet did not condemn her. No, Jesus offered her living water – the kind that does not run dry...eternal life through belief in Him.

This once invisible woman now became the center of attention for the good. She cared enough to tell the others – those who had once condemned her, to come see for themselves the goodness of the Lord.

🌸 **What does this story say to you about the thought of being invisible and how might it change your attitude this week?**

Well, friends, another day down. I hope God is speaking to you in some wonderful way about how loved you are and how great He is!

Father, there are times I feel invisible, but I know that You see me and that You find value in who I am. I pray that You will remind me today how much I am loved. Thank You, Lord. Amen.

See you tomorrow for Day 4!

Kristi

Pity Party Princess

Week 2 - Day 4

"Strong women don't play victim, don't make themselves look pitiful, and don't point fingers. They stand and they deal." – Mandy Hale

Welcome back! We are just rolling along like we own the place. ☺

Today we are going to talk about something we've probably all done at one time or another, but in all reality, a thing which accomplishes nothing more than deeper depression and exhaustion. I'm talking about the ultimate pity party. Anyone ever throw one of these?

Oh, we are good! At times, we can invite the guests, hang the decorations, and cook up a big ole dish of pity like none other's brother. I know, because I'm probably an expert at it. Lol.

There have been so many times when I felt as if God had left the building; like I was no longer important to my husband or kids; as if everyone else had these so-called "perfect" lives, and here I was just cleaning Kool-aid stains out of the carpet for the fifteenth time in a week. Relate?

Listen, girls, the enemy is so good about dancing all over our emotions. He can take an exhaustion-driven tone by our husband, an untimely circumstance (flat tire, broken hot water heater, etc.), an illness, etc., and cause us to feel as if we are on the Titanic going down to the darkest abyss. Do not listen to your feelings! They will lie to you every time.

Turn with me to the book of Jonah. This guy…we could call him a drama king for sure. Let's start with Chapter 4, and then answer the following:

(A little background: Jonah was a prophet called by God to go to the wicked Ninevites and tell them to repent or be annihilated. Jonah first refused, but was swallowed by a great fish until He realized he needed to do what God asked him to do.)

Why was Jonah feeling sorry for himself? (You might need to look back at Jonah 3:10)

Was Jonah justified in his actions? Why or why not?

What was his solution to his anger and resentment?

What was God's reaction to Jonah's pity party?

Okay, friends, from this story we see that sometimes life happens. We may be doing exactly what God has asked us to do and yet we're not happy. Maybe things aren't going so well and we feel as if we've been swallowed by a big ole stinky fish.

In the law enforcement world – in our marriages and relationships, not everything is going to go the way we want it to. Our officer may end up on continuous graveyard shifts limiting time and energy to do anything with friends or family, or your spouse may not get that promotion they worked so hard for, or perhaps the two of you have felt God calling you to move to a different department though it is miles away from everyone you know and love.

Whatever your present circumstance may be, sometimes things can't seem to gel for you. You begin to wonder why God has rested His favor on others but not on you. Listen, the joy does not come in the answer but in the journey.

Jonah missed the whole lesson God laid out before him because he was too concerned with his own comfort and desires. Unfortunately, we do the very same thing. I've seen so many posts on social media from wives and girlfriends upset over this or that - he didn't call or text back right away, he didn't want to talk once he got home, he seems to spend more time in the squad car than in the family car, and what do they do? They bring out the party hats and horns while serving up a big ole dish of poor me.

- ✹ How do you think God responds to that type of attitude? What are some steps you and I can take when we are tempted to feel sorry for ourselves?

Pick one of the following set of verses and summarize them in the space below. Let's make this a challenge to ourselves over the coming weeks and see how differently we feel and respond as we take our eyes off self and put them where they belong…on God! Say it with me, "No more parties!"

Psalm 37:3-4   Hebrews 12:5-11   Hebrews 12:1-3   Psalm 42:5

Eyes on Him, sweet one. No party is ever complete until Jesus is the guest of honor.

See you tomorrow.

Kristi

Discovering the Big "C"...Contentment

Week 2 - Day 5

> *"A harvest of peace is produced from a seed of contentment."* – Unknown

Hello again, my sweet friend! I'm so glad you are sticking with me on this crazy journey. This whole week has been focused on one of the downsides of law enforcement life – loneliness and all that comes with it.

Today as we close out this part of the study, I want to zoom in on the big "C" word - contentment. Ugh. I have to say that I have struggled with this one more than any other. The good thing is, God knows our struggles, and has provided quite a bit of commentary in His Word. When we are alone, our needs are being overlooked for whatever reason, and things may or may not be going the way we'd like. Those are the times we often begin a search for something to meet our longing. Yet, the Bible tells us that we need to learn to be content in *all* situations; to find *Him* and make *Him* the center of our lives, which in turn will help curb that ferocious appetite for other things.

Let's take a look, shall we?

Read each of the following verses about contentment and answer the question after each verse.

I know what it is to be in need, and I know what it is to have plenty. I have learned the secret of being content in any and every situation, whether well fed or hungry, whether living in plenty or in want. I can do all this through him who gives me strength. Philippians 4:12-13

What do you think is the "secret" Paul is talking about?

Keep your lives free from the love of money and be content with what you have, because God has said, "Never will I leave you; never will I forsake you." Hebrews 13:5

What is God's promise to us whether we have much or little?

But godliness with contentment is great gain. For we brought nothing into the world, and we can take nothing out of it. 1 Timothy 6:6-7

What is the value God places on our "stuff"?

Then he said to them, "Watch out! Be on your guard against all kinds of greed; life does not consist in an abundance of possessions." Luke 12:15

What do you think life is really all about?

That is why, for Christ's sake, I delight in weaknesses, in insults, in hardships, in persecutions, in difficulties. For when I am weak, then I am strong. 2 Corinthians 12:10

What do our trials teach us?

These verses are sometimes difficult to swallow. Trust me, I've been married to a cop for almost 29 years. We've known more years of hardship financially, than abundance. I've experienced the loneliness and restlessness of being a cop's wife. I can think back to times when out of sheer boredom, I would head to the store to buy something I could probably live without, or express emphatically to my husband, our "need" for bigger toys we really couldn't afford.

But there's even more than just material things when learning the lesson of contentment.

Contentment is something we need deep within our soul. Too many times, we feel as if we are missing out on something, so we begin a search to find that which fulfill us. Some will look for it in a new career, a hobby, circle of friends, education level, hair color, piece of clothing or accessory, or at worst, even a new love interest. *But unfortunately, there is nothing we can obtain here on this earth that will completely satisfy.* Oh, we may feel great for awhile, but eventually the newness and excitement will wear off, and that deep seated longing will return with a vengeance.

♣ So let me ask you…have you ever struggled with a lack of contentment? If so, what do you think set it off and how did you handle it?

The Apostle Paul talked about contentment in Philippians 4, as he explained learning to be at peace with whatever situation he might be experiencing. Paul knew contentment in hardships –

beatings, a stoning, a shipwreck, attempts on his life, imprisonments, etc., but he also befriended it in prosperous times.

Read the following verse then circle the words or phrase(s) describing Paul's mindset about whatever situation he may encounter.

Brothers, I do not consider myself yet to have laid hold of it. But one thing I do: Forgetting what is behind and straining toward what is ahead, I press on toward the goal to win the prize of God's heavenly calling in Christ Jesus. Philippians 3:13-14

Friend, I pray that even in those times when you and I are feeling alone…perhaps unimportant or overlooked, instead of wrestling against it by looking for something or someone else to fulfill us, my hope is that we will "press on" hard after God. He's the only One who can bring that total contentment.

In closing, read the following words as if they were written directly to you. Your Heavenly Daddy is crazy about you! I hope you know that. ☺

Dear Child,

I know this life you live can be lonely and burdensome; the stresses more than you can bear at times, but I have placed you here for a purpose. You were created for such a time as this.

In those moments when you feel alone, remember, I am always by your side. Spend time with Me. You are my precious child and I want for you to come to Me and lay your burdens at My feet.

There are so many things in this world that beckon for your attention, but what I can give you will last far beyond what any of these frivolous tokens can.

Today, don't wait! When those old feelings of frustration and emptiness begin to take hold, say My name and I will calm your troubled soul. You are so dearly loved!

Thinking of you always,

Your Heavenly Daddy

See you next week!

Kristi

A Note From a Police Wife...

It was just like any other evening, doing our normal routine. We were getting ready for bed when my husband got a phone call. I could hear his end of the conversation and knew what was coming. He told me he had to go, that there was an active shooter. We live in a very small town, and I can't say I ever remember hearing of an active shooter in my 30 years of living here.

I immediately start praying. I didn't know what was going on exactly, but I knew it wasn't good. I texted a good police wife friend and began to stalk some of the Facebook groups that I saw talking about it. There was a man shooting out of his upstairs townhouse window. Many people were evacuated, and thankfully no one was hurt that we knew of. I tried to find a police radio app that would work with his department, but with no luck. It was probably a good thing, because I soon found out this man had a child in his bedroom with him. Lord only knows what was going on with that child. Were they dead? Alive?

Now, I know my husband – a member of the SWAT team, and I knew that he was not going to sit back and direct traffic. He was going to find some way to take that man down. I heard they were bringing the TX DPS SWAT team in from Ft. Worth and Austin (7 and 3 hours away). The fear trying to enter my mind was indescribable. Was this going to be the night? How many casualties were we going to have? Was my husband going to be the one to possibly kill him? How would we handle that if it happened?

I kept reminding myself of the things I would say when he was deployed to Iraq or Afghanistan; no news is good news. I just knew in my spirit I had to pray for him, for the officers involved, and for wisdom. I couldn't even put it into words sometimes, but I knew it was not a good situation.

It was hours before I heard anything from him. Other wives were getting texts from their husbands. Why not me? One husband told his wife to tell me that my husband loved me and he was okay. Just knowing that helped tremendously.

Reading the posts on Facebook was not a good idea. People in the area were reporting shots fired, the cops making them stay in their homes, and the rumors...oh, the rumors. I had no idea what was actually happening. Was it over? How much longer was this going to go on?

Finally after a ton of chaos and confusion and prayer, we got word that the man had committed suicide in his room, and the baby was asleep the whole time (praise God).

I think I realized a lot about myself that night. I wholeheartedly learned that no matter what happens to my husband, I KNOW God will take care of me. If that was my last day with him, I would be very thankful for the times we had together. The thought of planning the funeral and being a widow were so hard to keep away from my mind, but I knew I just had to leave it all in God's hands. ~ Alicia Brooks

Week 3 – Day 1

He who finds a wife finds what is good and receives favor from the LORD. Proverbs 18:22

Well, friend, here we are on Week 3! Time passes quickly when you are having fun, eh?

This week we are going to focus on the whole package – the law enforcement marriage. Yes, we've talked about some of the hard issues, but because this is one of those professions with an extremely high divorce rate, I think it necessary to concentrate on the marriage itself.

> ❦ **What would you say is the hardest part of being married to the badge? Please describe below.**

In my book, *Under Fire: Marriage Through the Eyes of a Cop's Wife*, I cover all the stress factors which can cause hardship in a marriage…things like financial issues, politics, disappointment, loneliness, isolation, lack of communication, and even more serious things such as alcoholism, drug abuse, pornography, abuse, etc.

Today's lesson, however, I want to focus on the *good* aspects of law enforcement life; the positives of a godly marriage. Yes, there *are* many couples out there who see their marriage situation through different lenses. Does that mean they never have problems? Nah, but they've learned over time how to make it work. They've found the key to marital harmony regardless of some of the ups and downs that come with a stressful occupation such as this.

Let's take a look at one such couple: Derrek and Heidi Hogan…

> The Lord has been so faithful, merciful, and long-suffering as we learned how to make our marriage work. It took me, as a wife, several years to embrace God's design of the man spiritually leading the family, and coming up under my husband as the head of our home. We also both realized that in order to bring glory to Christ, we had to sacrificially set aside ourselves, essentially dying to our own flesh, so that we may become united to further His kingdom. You see, marriage and life are not really about us, but about what honors God because He alone is worthy. Sure, we still have disagreements, but we choose our words carefully, see the best in the other, and are quick to apologize and forgive. Our marriage is thriving now as we abide in Him, giving endless grace to and loving one another without boundaries.

So, in looking at Heidi's testimony, we see there is one key ingredient in a successful marriage – God. He created marriage, and He is the One who can sustain your marriage. Without Him in the equation, well…it simply has more opportunity to shatter into a million pieces.

What do you believe are some key essentials for a great marriage and why?

How does your marriage rate? Read the statement, then circle the number that best describes where you and your spouse are in your marital relationship, 1 being the lowest and 10 being the highest.

In our marriage, there is an equal amount of give and take in reference to love, affection, time, etc.

1   2   3   4   5   6   7   8   9   10

In our marriage, we communicate well with each other.

1   2   3   4   5   6   7   8   9   10

In our marriage, both of us are equally committed to the Lord and seek to serve Him daily.

1   2   3   4   5   6   7   8   9   10

In our marriage, we make sure to not go to bed angry with one another and always try to work out our differences.

1   2   3   4   5   6   7   8   9   10

In our marriage, we both seek to put the other's needs before our own.

1   2   3   4   5   6   7   8   9   10

In our marriage, we take time to pray together as a couple.

1   2   3   4   5   6   7   8   9   10

Okay, so how did you do? How is your marriage stacking up? Is there room for improvement or are you one of those who seem to have it all together?

Whether you have a terrific marriage with very little conflict, or your marriage is spiraling out of control, there is always room for improvement and always hope! Let's dig in and see what God has to say about our relationships.

Look up the following verses on the left hand side, and then list the essential quality (ies) on the right side. These qualities are vital to a healthy marital relationship.

Passage	Quality/Qualities Needed
John 13:34-35	_____
Mark 10:6-9	_____
Proverbs 5:18-19	_____
Ephesians 5:21-22	_____
Ephesians 5:33	_____
1 Peter 3:2	_____
1 Corinthians 13:4-7	_____
Hebrews 10:24-25	_____

Okay, so there is a lot of information here – some directly related to marriage and others in general for believers. However, all of it, if put into practice, will benefit our marital relationship.

For your homework assignment after today's lesson, I want you to look back at how you rated your marriage (the exercise of choosing between 1 and 10) then look over what you just listed as qualities every marriage should encompass.

If there are areas in need of some work, then jot a few notes below and spend time with the Father. This life we are living really *can* be a badge of honor, a true match made in Heaven, if *He* is in control.

Hugs to you, sweet friend. See you tomorrow.

Kristi

For Better or Worse

Week 3 - Day 2

More marriages might survive if the partners realized that sometimes the better comes after the worse. – Doug Larson

Marriage can sometimes get comfortable with the worse and forget about the better, can't it? Welcome back and hope you are ready to tackle the frayed ends of marriage…the crux of what it's all about – hanging in there no matter what.

Let's take a look at the very beginning when God first created marriage. Join with me as we read…

> "The LORD God said, 'It is not good for the man to be alone. I will make a helper suitable for him.'…But for Adam no suitable helper was found. So the LORD God caused the man to fall into a deep sleep; and while he was sleeping, he took one of the man's ribs and closed up the place with flesh. Then the LORD God made a woman from the rib he had taken out of the man, and he brought her to the man…For this reason a man will leave his father and mother and be united to his wife, and they will become one flesh." Genesis 2:18, 20b-22, 24

God created marriage. He literally formed the first woman from the first man's rib and told them to unite and become one flesh. Think about it…one became two, and two became one. They were two separate individuals created to be one unit.

So what does this mean in terms of our marriage today?

God has brought together you and your spouse, as created separate individuals, with different personalities, talents, giftedness, likes and dislikes, but together you are one in the sight of God and man. Meaning, you function together as a unit…as a team…on the same overall page, working for the same purpose.

But what happens when part of the team is non-functioning? What happens when one half drops off and pulls away from the wholeness of the unit?

Unfortunately, especially in this profession, there is a lot of that. For whatever reason, whether it be stress, PTSD, extra outside pressures, temptations, or just plain ole sinful choices, there are many couples who will face that breaking away of one of the partners. This is one of those factors considered as "the worse" in marriage. However, let's not forget, we repeated vows that said for better *or* worse. We promised we would stay in the fight no matter what. We would hang in there until the last nail was in the coffin. We would hold up the battle flag until there was no shred of material left to wave in the breeze. We would stand.

Think of a time in your marriage when you felt as if you were the only one standing or fighting. If you can, share your thoughts below:

Let's take a look at a story when one couple was certainly dealing with the "worse". **Turn to and read 1 Samuel 25:1-44.**

Names some qualities you see in Abigail in dealing with a husband who almost brought destruction on their household.

Now turn to Proverbs 31:10-31 and list qualities of a godly wife/mother:

Do you believe Abigail was displaying some of these characteristics? Why or why not?

What difference(s) do you see between Abigail and the Proverbs 31 woman in reference to their husband's attitudes towards them?

Okay, so let's take a look back at what we read, and I'll try and explain my pattern of thinking.

Abigail was dealing with a husband who was "surly and mean". Perhaps he hadn't always been this way. It's possible that when they first began the courtship process, Nabal was attentive and loving towards her. Yet, over time, this man's true colors began to shine through.

He had become selfish and full of pride. Even though kindness had been shown to him indirectly through his shepherds and herds of sheep, Nabal thought of no-one else, but Nabal. His self-centered attitude, ended up being his own undoing, and Abigail was left picking up the pieces of a one-sided relationship, dodging bullets brought on by her husband's attitude, and keeping peace when all things under heaven were about to hit the fan. Can anyone relate?

Unfortunately, Nabal did not recognize the measure of his own sin nor the value of his wife until it was too late.

Now let's contrast that to the Proverbs 31 woman.

This woman, like Abigail, was wise. She was a woman of action and decision. Within all the projects she undertook and godly characteristics she put on, this woman was revered and praised by her husband. He understood what a treasure he had been gifted with and he lacked nothing of value.

Friend, it boils down to this…you or I may have been dealt a Nabal in this marriage of ours. Hopefully we are *not* the Nabal!

Perhaps, though, you are totally blessed with a Proverbs 31 husband who respects, loves and admires you! For that, be thankful!

However, whichever type of spouse or marriage we are in, we have a responsibility to display the characteristics of Abigail and the Proverbs 31 woman. We are to be women of action, wise, confident, generous, efficient, courageous, prosperous, well-spoken, strong, and noble. Because when you and I are doing our best to live out what God has created us to be, then His blessings will see us through.

This doesn't mean that our marriages will be perfect or that we will never walk through fire, but what it does mean is that He will be there right beside us, guiding us through wherever we walk.

- What are some ways you can bless your spouse today by displaying some of the qualities we've just discussed?

I hope this lesson has challenged you just a bit. You know, it's never easy being in a one-sided relationship, but when we can put our focus on God and allow Him to empower us in being the best wife and person we can be, slowly all those faults we once found in our spouse become a little less prominent. They are no longer the ones creating or destroying our happiness, for our true joy comes from the Lord!

See you tomorrow.

Kristi

Hitch Up the Team, Margaret!

Week 3 - Day 3

> *"Coming together is the beginning. Keeping together is progress. Working together is success."* – Henry Ford

This past October, Rick and I were the keynote speakers at a law enforcement retreat in Ontario, Canada. On Saturday, we had several hours of free time that if we desired, could be spent playing a version of The Amazing Race.

I'm always up for a challenge, so thought it would be fun to pair up with another couple, work as a team, and fulfill all the requirements set before us. Our team quickly found out that not everyone works at the same pace, is as athletic or agile as others, nor has the drive without a lot of prodding to finish. Yet, finish we did…in seventh place! Not Olympic material, but not too bad for old folks. Ha!

Marriage is all about teamwork, and like we discussed in yesterday's lesson, if one person is MIA, then it makes the whole unit begin to sink.

Today, I want to take a look at what the Bible has to say about being part of a team. **Read the following verses and circle the phrase, word, etc. that describes the positives of working together.**

"Two are better than one, because they have a good reward for their toil. For if they fall, one will lift up his fellow. But woe to him who is alone when he falls and has not another to lift him up! Again, if two lie together, they keep warm, but how can one keep warm alone? And though a man might prevail against one who is alone, two will withstand him—a threefold cord is not quickly broken." Ecclesiastes 4:9-12

"Iron sharpens iron, and one man sharpens another." Proverbs 27:17

"May the God of endurance and encouragement grant you to live in such harmony with one another, in accord with Christ Jesus, that together you may with one voice glorify the God and Father of our Lord Jesus Christ." Romans 15:5-6

"Then the Lord God said, "It is not good that the man should be alone; I will make him a helper fit for him." Genesis 2:18

"Bear one another's burdens, and so fulfill the law of Christ." Galatians 6:2

Friend, when we incorporate teamwork in our marriage, things get done and done properly! We were not created to do this life alone. We need others and part of that "others" is our spouse.

❦ Think of a time you and your spouse worked together on something. It might have been a particular project, or setting up rules for your children, cleaning up the kitchen after dinner, or something totally fun. What was the outcome? How did you feel working beside each other?

Marriage is all about teamwork. To keep the relationship afloat, both are going to have to invest time and energy in keeping it fresh and alive.

If you have children, then teamwork as parents is definitely a necessity! Those little creatures can completely exhaust the energy of both, let alone one parent. Yet, as a law enforcement family, the team is often separated by duty, stress, energy, further training, or other situations, making the marriage lopsided and causing strain.

What are some ways you can make sure you and your spouse stay on the same page and strengthen the team, despite all the difficulties of law enforcement life?

Rick and I were married in 1988 after dating all throughout high school. We were a whopping eighteen and nineteen years old when we married (too young), and right away began adding children. By the time Rick completed academy at age twenty-one, life was already crazy with both of us working full-time jobs, swing shifts, a toddler in tow, and another baby on the way. Our teamwork was not so much about working together as it was simply surviving. After about six or seven years, the continuing break down came to a head, and the team was almost non-existent. That's when we finally realized we had a choice between a.) Getting back in the game with *Someone* other than ourselves calling the shots, or b.) Call it quits. Thankfully, we allowed that Someone…God, to take over. He had a lot of cleaning up to do, but it was worth it! We will be celebrating our 29th anniversary this July. ☺

Let's take a look at some ways we can promote that team spirit in our marriage. Match the scripture on the left with the activity on the right.

Colossians 3:13   Encourage one another

Ephesians 4:2   Forgive

James 5:16   Enjoy or rejoice in one another sexually

Proverbs 5:18   Pray for each other

1 Thessalonians 5:11   Be humble, gentle and PATIENT with each other

Well, friend, the bottom line for a successful marriage is a team of three – you, your spouse, and God. If you have this equation in place, you're bound to succeed. I'm going to leave you with a pyramid drawing I use in my marriage seminars. Study it. Show it to your spouse. For Pete's sake, cut it out and hang it up somewhere. As each of us draw closer to God, we are in essence drawing closer to each other. Voila! A winning team!

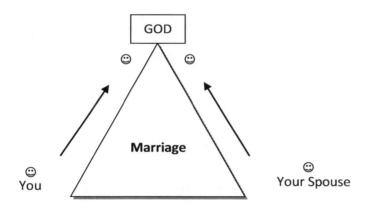

Have a great rest of the day. See you tomorrow.

Kristi

Running the Race; Racing to Win

Week 3 - Day 4

"When your legs can't run anymore, run with your heart." - Unknown

Are you feeling the burn? Is the time you are putting into this study strengthening you at all, or is it just making you plain ole tired?

Today we are going to look at running the race. Marriage is a lot like a race, and the Bible tells us that the Christian faith is definitely like a race. Both of these take time, patience, work and a lot of prayer, yet both are so worth the effort.

What happens to a runner if he or she never trains or practices?

What are some ways runners prepare for a big race?

A friend of ours is a runner. It is nothing for her to get up in the morning and run ten miles before she goes to work! I'm sure she would tell you, though, this ability did not come overnight. She had to make her body get up and run…when it was raining, when it was cold, in the heat, and even when she didn't feel well. She eats foods that give her energy without causing her to crash. She has worked at running small amounts so that over time, she has become able to run marathon levels.

When we consider our marriage, we must realize that it takes work and time and preparation, daily. We have to keep our eyes on the prize, knowing that whatever we put into it, will come back to us. The key component to surviving this law enforcement life and becoming an example to others, is our relationship with Christ.

Read the following verses about running a race. Underline the word "race" in each verse. Circle the action verbs such as "run", "fought", "finished", etc. Highlight or draw parenthesis around the reason for running or finishing the race.

However, I consider my life worth nothing to me; my only aim is to finish the race and complete the task the Lord Jesus has given me—the task of testifying to the good news of God's grace. Acts 20:24

Do you not know that in a race all the runners run, but only one gets the prize? Run in such a way as to get the prize. 1 Corinthians 9:24

I have fought the good fight, I have finished the race, I have kept the faith. Now there is in store for me the crown of righteousness, which the Lord, the righteous Judge, will award to me on that day—and not only to me, but also to all who have longed for his appearing. 2 Timothy 4:7-8

Therefore, since we are surrounded by such a great cloud of witnesses, let us throw off everything that hinders and the sin that so easily entangles. And let us run with perseverance the race marked out for us, fixing our eyes on Jesus, the pioneer and perfecter of faith. For the joy set before him he endured the cross, scorning its shame, and sat down at the right hand of the throne of God. Hebrews 12:1-2

🐾 As you read these verses, are there any promises here that help us to not only focus on our spiritual lives, but could help us in our marriages as well?

How are marriages focused on Christ different from the world?

Jamie married her high school sweetheart. Chad had gone into the military right after graduation and the two had made the best of all the army had to offer – the separation period during basic training, base assignment, being away from family and friends, and one overseas tour. In their late twenties/early thirties, Chad got out of the service and began his law enforcement career. The couple had not put much time or thought into church or anything God related during their military stint, yet, after Chad's academy and subsequent hiring at a large department, Jamie began to realize something was missing in their relationship. Though they had a pretty good marriage, they both seemed to have that emptiness despite being reunited with family and those they loved. Not long after, Jamie was invited to a Bible study with a couple of other police wives in her husband's department. Reluctant at first, she finally submitted to attend one of the meetings and find out what all the hub bub was. After several weeks of encouragement and prayer support from friends, Jamie understood that she and Chad had let their guard down; they had fallen out of the race and had no real blueprint to build marriage the right way. She was now ready to focus on God and allow Him to fill in the missing pieces.

What happens when we submit to God in our marriage?

Does submitting to Him mean that we will never have problems? Why or why not?

Friend, I know it seems as if I'm pounding this God drum over and over and over. Maybe I am. Yet, I know from experience, that a marriage without a firm foundation in Him will be more likely to fail than one firmly planted.

Before we close out today's lesson, I want to take a look at a couple who had it going on. These two were running the race together and the Lord had His hand of blessing on them. Let's take a look.

Read the following accounts of Priscilla and Aquilla, then answer the questions.

Acts 18:1-7, 18-21, 24-28; 1 Corinthians 16:19; Romans 16:1-5

- **Who were Priscilla and Aquilla?**

- **How involved were they in the life of Paul, in the life of the church, and in the lives of fellow believers?**

- **How does their faith and "togetherness in the Lord", speak to you and your spouse/marriage?**

These two loved the Lord first and each other second. They made it their mission to serve God and help others every opportunity given to them. Was their marriage perfect? Though the scriptures do not give us a close up of their day to day lives, I'm assuming that they had their moments of frustrations and disappointments like every other marriage. The difference from so many others is that they served the Lord together, and that was the glue that bound them as a couple.

The point of today's lesson is not about what is right or wrong with your marriage. The point is, that a marriage carefully crafted, with God as the center, will almost always follow the path of continual redemption and grace.

My prayer for you is that your marriage, if not already, will find opportunity to serve the Lord together. Like the old expression says, "A family that prays together, stays together."

Blessings,

Kristi

Thoughts...

Leaving a Legacy

Week 3 - Day 5

> *"Leave a spiritual legacy in your family, or you will leave no legacy at all."* – Unknown

What is a legacy? How do we leave one? In all reality, you and I are leaving a legacy for those around us whether we realize it or not.

Today, we are going to end this week's study on marriage by talking about the footprints we leave on this earth, both good and bad.

As a law enforcement wife, I have observed my husband fulfill his duties as an officer to the best of his God-given abilities. He has tried to treat each individual with respect as a fellow human being, despite the fact he or she may come under discipline within his authority, as an officer of the law.

I have witnessed him listening to a single mom pour her heart out over an unruly teenager, or a young runaway listing all the reasons why she/he can't go home.

This man of mine has wrestled with a woman who held a loaded gun to her own abdomen and has literally stood between a woman and the demons who taunted her.

As officers, our men and women leave footprints on the lives of every person they deal with throughout their careers, but as often happens, the legacies left within the home have the greatest impact.

If we have children, our marriage is setting the example for our children's future. Those impressionable individuals are taking in every word spoken, every loving touch they observe, and every standard which is set. That, my friend, is a huge, HUGE responsibility that you and I have as parents within our marriage and within our home.

Let's take a look at some verses that talk about leaving a legacy.

You shall love the LORD your God with all your heart and with all your soul and with all your might. And these words that I command you today shall be on your heart. You shall teach them diligently to your children, and shall talk of them when you sit in your house, and when you walk by the way, and when you lie down, and when you rise. Deuteronomy 6:5-7

But lay up for yourselves treasures in heaven, where neither moth nor rust destroys and where thieves do not break in and steal. For where your treasure is, there your heart will be also. Matthew 6:20-21

For I am already being poured out as a drink offering, and the time of my departure has come. I have fought the good fight, I have finished the race, I have kept the faith. Henceforth there is laid up for me the crown of righteousness, which the Lord, the righteous judge, will award to me on that Day, and not only to me but also to all who have loved his appearing. 2 Timothy 4:6-8

But the steadfast love of the LORD is from everlasting to everlasting on those who fear him, and his righteousness to children's children... Psalm 103:17

Praise the LORD! Blessed is the man who fears the LORD, who greatly delights in his commandments! His offspring will be mighty in the land; the generation of the upright will be blessed. Wealth and riches are in his house, and his righteousness endures forever. Psalm 112:1-3

What are some characteristics of those who leave a legacy of faith to generations who follow?

How do these differ from what we see in today's society?

Does this challenge you in your own home and marriage? Why or why not?

Leaving a legacy is more than just living well. To leave a lasting legacy, is to build a foundation that will stand the test of time. How do we do that? We anchor ourselves to the Cornerstone – Jesus Christ.

  ❦ **Has there been someone in your life who left a lasting legacy which truly impacted you for the good? Explain.**

In 1988, Rick and I were in our late teens, newly married and pregnant with our first child. Because we had been raised in the church, we joined a church of our own and began attending a young married couple's class. Though most of the couples had a few years on us and were in their mid twenties and above, they helped encourage us tremendously in those early years. As time went on, Rick joined the police department, we had another child and our marriage began to struggle. The teachers of our class, a couple in their late thirties, mentored us and literally helped to save our marriage. Without their continuous outpouring of love into our lives, we probably would not have made it. The legacy they left us…the footprints they made on our life, left lasting impressions that hopefully we have been able to pass on to others.

Being the spouse of a police officer, you've probably heard the statistics of law enforcement marriage which ranges anywhere from 65-80% divorce rate. This life is not easy. There are many factors that can contribute to stresses and problems within the marital relationship, and unfortunately, many do not make it.

However, what couples forget in the process of all the mess and the anger and the bitterness of a broken covenant, is the legacy they are leaving for their children and others watching the breakdown of a God-ordained entity.

Wounds from a broken home run deep, and often spill over onto future relationships, yet, the good news is that with God's help, the most broken lives…those still licking the wounds of home grown battles, can be utterly changed and redirected. The seeds you have sown up to this point can be transformed into the most beautiful creation.

If you have found yourself as a participant or a product of a broken relationship, take heart. Our God is so much bigger than that. Allow Him to begin the transformation process and lay a new legacy down which will be like a beacon of light for weary travelers.

It is my prayer that this week has offered some hope and light to marriages in a challenging profession. To end this day and week's lesson, I'd like to share a poem I wrote. May it be your prayer today.

It's Not My Own

I'm on a journey; it's not my own.
A weary traveler far from home.
A well-worn highway many have trod;
A mate beside me, a gift from God.
Though we may stumble and fail to see
We're leaving footprints – a legacy.
A kind word spoken, a sweet embrace,
Forgiving spirit and smiling face.
I'll offer these in this life I've known
For this path I walk is not my own,
It belongs to Him and Him alone.
Thank you, God for marriage.

Blessings,

Kristi

A Note from a Police Wife...

Often we have to make sacrifices on the holidays. Like most other wives of police officers, I spend many holidays alone. One year my husband had to work Christmas Day, but was off the day after. We moved all our traditions, except mass, to the next day. It was so much fun and because the kids are older, they understood the changes. Christmas Day I spent most of it alone, but I had that extra day to myself to wrap gifts and prep for our amazing celebration the next day.

Ruth Kelly

*The life of a law enforcement family can be stressful, but the key to success and harmony, is finding creative ways to make memorable moments.

Duty Calls

Week 4 - Day 1

> *"Those who have the privilege to know have the duty to act."* – Albert Einstein

Welcome to our last week! Isn't it good to know you are about to complete something? I never like to leave anything half done. I want to finish it and check it off the list.

So continuing on, I've named this lesson "Duty Calls". I've left you with a quote from Albert Einstein, one of the greatest physicists of all times.

What do you think he meant when talking about duty?

How can we apply that to our lives as the spouse of a police officer?

Here's how I see it. According to Romans 13, police officers and other enforcers of the law have been established by God. They have been called to this position to keep order and promote peace. You and I as wives of officers are also called.

Talk to anyone outside of law enforcement, and try as they may, they simply cannot understand what it's like to be a part of the law enforcement community. They do not grasp the fears and the responsibilities. It is hard for them to fathom the frustrations we feel or the hurt we experience when another "brother or sister" is killed in the line of duty, assaulted, abused, or otherwise mistreated. They do not understand the loneliness and the stresses we face on a daily basis. They just cannot.

Yet, God has created us – you and me, for this very purpose! We are strong for the task. Our love for our spouse is cemented to and wrapped within the thin blue line. We are loyal and proud of the men and women who serve our communities. We stand together in solidarity when one falls and (hopefully) support those left behind.

We have knowledge about the inner workings of our law enforcement. We see the personal side of our officer – the side no-one else is privy to. We understand their hurts and see them when they are at their breaking point. And…it is in our power and it is our duty to act. We are women of action, not passive wallflowers. So what is our duty? Glad you asked! Before we get to that, let's first look at what our husband's duty is.

Turn to and read Romans 13:1-5, then answer the questions.

Who is called to submit to our governing authorities?

Who establishes these authorities?

What happens if people rebel against these authorities?

What are the responsibilities of those in authority?

Pretty clear instructions, ay? Authority is instituted by God, and those He raises up to these positions have the responsibility to keep order and peace, but to also bring wrath for those who come against them.

However, there is a part to this passage that we don't find here. If it were described, it might illustrate how authorities at times, break down. They experience horrific things and witness devastation and terror that no man, woman or child should ever experience.

They often have nightmares and become hardened and cynical; hollow and cold, and it takes a special kind of partner to recognize and separate strains of the job versus the true inner character. The spouse has to be willing to love them and be available even when hard times come.

I want to take you to a passage in the Bible which will require you to step out of your box and put yourself in the position of an imaginary character. Sounds risky, doesn't it?

Turn with me and read Luke 23:26-49. Focus in on verse 47. Imagine for a moment that you are the wife of this man. The Bible does not say that he was married, nor does it give any information about him other than he was a Roman Centurion (soldier/keeper of the peace). Yet, imagine what he had witnessed and participated in that day...the trial, the scourging, the procession to Golgotha where they crucified an innocent man, the supernatural darkness, final act of forgiveness, tearing of the temple curtain, earthquakes, and finally, the death of our Lord.

What would have been your first action towards your husband at shift's end?

How do you think all these events affected this Centurion?

❧ **Understanding the enormity of this man's situation, would it change the way you respond to him or perhaps cause you to react differently? Why or why not?**

Okay, so I know that was a complete stretch, but what I wanted you to see are a couple of things:

1) Due to their profession, our husbands will be faced with some complex and extremely difficult situations where we may be the only one who takes the time to listen and offer comfort.
2) We will not and cannot truly understand what they've experienced, but we can make ourselves available. They may not open up to us, but we can provide them a "safe haven" to come home to.

Well, I hope this little escapade got you thinking in a different way. Our spouse experiences things we can never completely understand and those experiences can sometimes create tensions within the marital relationship. The support, love, and understanding you and I show them through these troubled times can make a world of difference.

Dear Father, please give me discernment to perceive those times when my spouse is struggling from a stressful situation. Give me wisdom to know what to say, how to say it, or when to just be silent. Help me to not allow those feelings of self, take over and crowd out understanding and love. Thank You! In Your precious name. Amen.

See you tomorrow friend.

Kristi

Combating the Distractions

Week 4 - Day 2

"Be about actions, not distractions." - Unknown

Distractions: They can come in many forms and fashion, anywhere from a sick child to an overly packed schedule. For our LEOs, distraction can cost him his marriage, his job and even his life, that's why as wives we must be diligent in our prayer and petition for our husbands.

Below I have listed different types of distractions and verses that pertain. Look up each one and answer the questions.

Distraction of Weariness/Lack of Sleep:

Matthew 11:28 – Who are we to turn to and what does He promise?

Isaiah 40:29 – What other things does He promise to give?

Hebrews 12:3 – Who are we to "consider" and why?

Colossians 1:29 – What does it say that is working in us?

Dear God, please give my husband rest along with Your strength and power, and always help him to keep his focus on You.

Distraction of Unhealthy Lifestyle Choices (improper nutrition, smoking, lack of exercise, etc.):

1 Corinthians 6:19-20 – What does scripture say about our body?

1 Corinthians 10:13 – What does it say about temptation?

Genesis 1:29 – As far as food, what is a good food source that God has given us?

Dear God, I thank You for my husband and ask that You help him value "Your temple". I ask that You give him wisdom to eat properly and make wise choices as to what he puts into his body. Help him to see the importance of taking care of what You have blessed him with, so that he brings You honor.

Distraction of Anxiety/Fear:

Isaiah 41:10 – What does God tell us in this passage about fear? What is His promise?

Philippians 4:6-7 – Instead of caving to fear, what are we called to do?

2 Timothy 1:7 – Where do you think the spirit of fear comes from and what does God give to us?

1 Peter 5:7 – We are to cast our fears on God? Why?

Dear God, bless my husband with full confidence and assurance that You are with him each and every moment. Please remove the spirit of fear and anxiety away from him and replace it with a spirit of courage and strength.

Distraction of Pain (both physical and mental):

Isaiah 53:3 – How can this verse bring us comfort?

Revelation 21:4 – Is there a solution or end to pain? Explain.

Romans 8:18 – What does Paul say about our sufferings?

Dear God, I ask that You draw near my husband in times of pain both physically and mentally. Help him to realize that these things are temporary in the grand design of Your plan for our lives. Keep his eyes focused on You and bring joy within his sight.

Distraction of Anger:

Ephesians 4:26 – What should be your husband's response (your response) when feelings of anger well up inside?

Romans 12:19 – As an officer, there are often times our husbands feel anger or hatred towards those who do wrong. What does the Lord say about this?

Ephesians 4:31-32 – There are often grievances that arise within a department, friendship or marriage that can cause anger and bitterness. What does God say about how we should treat those who have wronged us?

Dear God, I pray that You will give my husband a spirit of forgiveness and love toward his co-workers, his friends, and especially me. Help him to be filled with a compassionate heart which is slow to anger and quick to forgive.

Distraction of Politics:

Romans 13:1 – Politics within a department/city/county can be tough to deal with. However, what does God say about those who are "in charge"?

1 Timothy 2:1-4 - Instead of allowing the politics to get to us, how are we (our husbands) supposed to react towards those over us?

Romans 13:7 – What are some other things we are to give to those who are making the rules?

1 Corinthians 11:1 – And finally, what is our best weapon of defense?

Dear God, when things get crazy and hard to handle within my husband's department or area of service, I pray that You give him wisdom, a calm spirit and a Christ-like attitude. Help him to show respect and honor to those You have placed in these positions, and may Your favor rest on his shoulders. In Your precious name, Amen.

Girls, it is not easy for any of us to overcome distractions, but we can do it through God's strength and the power of His Word. Keep praying for your husband (and you) and watch how God begins to answer those prayers!

Blessings,

Kristi

♣ P.S. What are some distractions that you face, and how do they affect your relationships with your husband, children and God? What steps can you take to help eliminate or minimize them?

Week 4 - Day 3

> *"Reckless words pierce like a sword, but the tongue of the wise*
> *brings healing."* Proverbs 12:18

As we are wrapping up our study this week on surviving *Above the Fray*, today I want to take a look at one of the number one complaints within an LE marriage – lack of communication.

Due to complete sensory overload and being on an emotional high for such long periods of time, a typical officer crashes upon re-entry of his home. Here he has entered his safety net and now shifts into idle mode in order to help process all he has experienced over the course of a shift.

Decision making comes to a standstill. Communication is sometimes non-existent. Mindless, almost mechanical behavior such as watching television, scrolling through the phone, game playing, etc. becomes routine.

So what is a wife to do? She is relational by nature and needs her man to reconnect in order to feel loved and secure.

I think in order to understand how we respond in this situation, we must first take a look at what our role is as a wife.

❦ **Read Proverbs 31:10-12. What do these scriptures tell us about a wife and her relationship to her husband?**

If you were to read the entire Proverbs 31 passage (vs. 10-31), you'd notice that it lists all the duties or tasks this wonder woman performs, yet, in verse 23, the writer slips in these words, **"Her husband is respected at the city gate, where he takes his seat among the elders of the land."** Why do you think the writer put that tidbit of information in there? What, if anything, does that have to do with her?

Look now at verse 31 where it reads, **"and let <u>her works</u> bring her praise at the city gate."** Who was it sitting at the city gate and highly respected? What are your thoughts here about any possible connection between her works and her husband?

Let's look at some other qualities of a godly wife. Read the following and list the quality or qualities beside it.

Ephesians 5:22-24

Ephesians 5:33b

Titus 2:4-5

1 Peter 3:1-5

1 Corinthians 7:2-5

Alright, now that we have a number of attributes of a godly wife, we can tackle the communication factor by utilizing the many different God-given qualities we have to effectively communicate with our husbands.

There are different types of communication within a marriage (or any relationship): **verbal, nonverbal (physical), visual, written**.

Because we recognize the fact that an officer deals with things no human being should ever have to deal with or see, then it is no wonder they shut down emotionally and have a hard time re-entering the "all-in, face-to-face, I'm opening up and being vulnerable" zone.

Let's look at each type of communication and find ways to effectively relate to our spouse within that category.

Verbal

Proverbs 15:1 – How much power do our words have on a conversation?

Ephesians 4:29 – What should the quality of our words be?

Psalm 141:3 – Do we always have to be talking?

Proverbs 12:18 – Put the word "nagging" in the place of "rash words". What does this tell you?

Proverbs 25:11 – How valuable are carefully crafted words?

Nonverbal

Matthew 7:12 – What is the challenge for us as wives/as Christians?

1 Peter 3:1 – How do our actions play a part in our husband's life? Even if our husband is a strong Christian, how can our actions speak louder than words?

Proverbs 18:13 – Listening more than we speak is a great tool in marriage. What does the Bible say about those who do not listen well?

Proverbs 5:15-19 – Nonverbal communication can also take place in the bedroom (and should!). How do you think your sexual expression of love to your husband helps open the lines of communication?

Visual

Go back and skim through Proverbs 31:10-31. Make a list of some of the visual ways this woman communicates her love for her husband and family.

Written

Psalm 119:105 - If God's Word is a lamp to our feet and a light to our path, how can we communicate and share it with our husband?

1 Thessalonians 5:11 – What are some ways you can encourage your husband and build him up?

All in all, I have found that true communication has responsibility on both parties. Husband and wife must make a conscious effort to carve out what I like to call "face time" – when the two can sit and talk together without the distraction of children, cell phones, television, etc. This is why date nights are crucial.

Though the stresses of law enforcement can stifle communication, it *can* be achieved and a couple *can* find creative ways to keep the lines of communication open. Hang in there. With God, all things are possible!

Later friend,

Kristi

Week 4 - Day 4

> *"A long-lasting marriage is built by two people who believe in – and live by – the solemn promise they made."* Darlene Schacht

Society today has become too accustomed to the words "temporary" and "disposable". If something quits working it simply gets tossed out and replaced with another. Gone are the days when we took time and ingenuity to fix what was broken or damaged. If the toaster breaks, we see it as replaceable. Voila! Perfect toast again....or is it?

Scouring through the internet, or talking with LEOs and their spouses across the nation, I often run across the ugly effects of "temporary marriages" which echo the skyrocketing statistics of 65-80% divorce rate.

I hear stories of broken homes, custody battles, MIA fathers and live-in lovers. How does this happen and is there a solution? The good news is YES! There is an answer and His name is *Jesus*.

Like the scripture says, *"A person standing alone can be attacked and defeated, but two can stand back-to-back and conquer. Three are even better, for a triple-braided cord is not easily broken."* God should be that middle cord. With Him in place, an LE marriage...any marriage can withstand even the toughest of circumstances. I know, I've lived it.

Below I've listed five ways to solidify your marriage and ensure that it is a permanent fixture. **Read the scriptures and answer the questions that go along with each item.**

1. Always keep God front and center in your marriage.

Genesis 2:18 – Why was marriage created?

Mark 10:6-9 – What happens when a man and woman "come together"?

Ephesians 5:30-33 – What relationship does earthly marriage symbolize?

When we keep God in the center of our marriage, He will bless it. Why? Because He created us one for another (male and female/husband and wife) to come together in sexual union and become one flesh, to procreate, and also represent an earthly picture of Christ and the church.

2. Prayer in marriage is vital.

James 5:16 – What does the Bible say about prayer?

1 Thessalonians 5:16-18 – What are 3 things God commands us to do, one of which is prayer? How should this affect your marriage?

Matthew 5:44 – When we are angry with our spouse (or anyone), what should we do?

Prayer is vital in marriage because it takes our focus off of self and places it 1.) On God and 2.) Onto our spouse. Even when we are angry, hurt or feel disconnected in our relationship, God calls us to pray, to be thankful and to rejoice in our circumstance. If we do these things, our feelings toward our spouse are liable to change for the better.

3. Laugh and have fun in your relationship.

Proverbs 17:22 – What is the comparison/contrast between joy and a crushed or depressed spirit? How do you think either one can affect your marriage?

Psalm 16:11 – Who is the supplier of joy and what does that tell you about the importance of God in your marriage/life?

Laughter is a must in marriage. If we fail to find the humor in things then our marriage will dry up and die. Law enforcement life especially needs that counter-balance to all the evil they incur. So what are you waiting for? Get your laughter on…act silly…enjoy your marriage! ☺

4. SEX! And plenty of it.

1 Corinthians 7:3-5 – What are we commanded to do/not to do, both husband and wife, and why?

Proverbs 5:18-19 – Ladies…how powerful is your love to your husband? (Hint: one word)

1 Corinthians 7:2 – (Regular) Sex between husband and wife is a protection against what?

Okay…so we're talking about the "S" word! Yes, ladies, it is a vital part of marriage. God created it and approves of it between a husband and wife. Matter-of-fact, did you realize that it is a part of worship? Yes, that's right. When we are displaying love to our husbands, it is being obedient to God and His commands. Therefore, obedience is a form of worship! Soooo…hurry up with this study, and then go find your man. Wink.

5. Work out your differences with one another.

🛡 Romans 12:18 – What are we supposed to do if at all possible, at all times?

John 13:34 - What overcomes all indifference or frustration – What are we commanded to do?

Proverbs 17:14 – What does the Bible say we are to do before a fight or disagreement breaks out?

Proverbs 19:11 – What is another thing God calls us to do when our spouse has wronged us?

Girls, it is not easy to overlook an offense and forgive. But we must remember how much we've been forgiven. Putting it into that perspective makes it a whole lot easier when it comes to our spouse and situations that are bound to arise. Love, forgive, overlook and stop before it starts. These are things that you can accomplish with God's help.

Remember that marriage is not easy, but it is so worth it. Our marriages *can* last a lifetime and we *can* withstand frustrations and aggravations that come our way, and love our man the way God intended us to. Chin up. Trust me…marriage is like a fine wine. It gets better with age and time. ☺

Until tomorrow…

Kristi

Insanity is Bliss

Week 4 - Day 5

"I don't suffer from insanity, I enjoy every minute of it." – *Unknown*

Insanity. That word has an array of other words to describe it - folly, lunacy, foolishness and madness. I have to admit there have been times in my marriage that I have felt as if I had been swallowed up by insanity. How about you?

I'm not saying that it is always like this. More times than not, the life Rick and I live just works for us, especially now that he has finally earned seniority with "normal" hours and our kids are grown and out of the house…sort of.

Yet, I remember those days when we met ourselves coming and going - the kids hardly seeing their dad throughout the week, and I continuously feeling like a single parent. Insanity. The word definitely could have fit our lives.

So how do we rise above it? How do we grab the reigns and come to acceptance? How do we settle in and live this life with grace?

First, we must believe God has chosen us for this role and will see us through it.

Jeremiah 29:11-13 – What do these verses tell you about your situation, and about God?

Second, we must believe that every hardship, struggle, frustration and trial are all points of strengthening in our character.

James 1:2-4 – What do our trials produce?

How can that quality help us in all aspects of our life?

Third, often the insanity we find ourselves in creates a desire for change to the better. If we stand strong and persevere, we receive rewards – a stronger marriage, a healthier home life, a stronger faith, etc.

James 1:12 – What does this scripture tell us that we will receive if we persevere?

Of course, this verse is talking about the perseverance through Christ, but isn't that the goal anyway? You may have heard the quote, "Happy life, happy wife", but let's change it to "Christ-filled life, happy wife". Yes…I like that better. Don't you?

> *I wasn't happy. My husband, though he tried, could not meet my needs and seemed to always come up short. Our kids drove me crazy. I quickly found out that patience was not one of my strong suits. My job was never enough and always seemed to be a source of stress in my life. I was like a restless wanderer who couldn't find a destination…that is until I found the Lord, or rather He found me.*

Can you relate at all? I hate to say it, but this was me for so many years. The stresses I brought on myself intermingled with the stresses of swing shifts, single parenting, lack of meaningful friendships, and a less-than-important relationship with the Lord caused me to quickly sink in all the chaos.

The key to surviving the stress factors, loneliness, apprehensions, frustrations, etc. is a strong foundation built on a relationship with the Lord. One way to build that foundation is through Bible study. What do the following verses remind us about being in God's Word?

Deuteronomy 6:6-7

1 Peter 3:15

2 Timothy 3:16-17

2 Timothy 2:15

Psalm 119:105

Isaiah 55:11

🏵 **Describe a situation which could have been handled better if you had been able to set your mind (and mouth) on a certain scripture or scriptures?**

I remember a particular incident when I did not handle my words and actions well and it cost me.

Rick and I had been married about ten years. I was tired of handling things on my own. I felt as if the kids and I had taken a back seat to police work. Then one afternoon, I had been pushed to the outer limits of reason. I needed a moment or ten on the front porch, away from my children. I had given them strict orders to *NOT* come outside unless someone was bleeding. It wasn't long when my darling middle son opened the door and bounced out of the house with the phone in his hand. A screaming tirade began as I had now been pushed over the cliff and was hurling to my emotional death. "I TOLD YOU TO STAY INSIDE!!! WHAT THE BLANK, BLANK, BLANK ARE YOU DOING?!!" Those words hung in the air like leaves on a windy day. My son looked at me wide-eyed and said meekly, "There's someone on the phone for you." Taking a step back, I realized that whoever was on the other end, heard the whole explosion. So, trying to do a little damage control, I straightened my back and picked up the phone, sweetly answering, "Hello?" There was a long pause then a click. I had officially left a forever negative impression not only on my young son, but also on one of our church members. Ugh.

Sometimes the stress of this life gets to us. We're human. I cannot say that we always handle things right, but somehow we do manage to survive. As I thought about and wrote this study, the whole point to be made is…persevere. Rise above. Plug into the One who can walk you through it effectively.

Living *above the fray* is hanging on for dear life when everything around you is crashing to the ground.

Sweet friend, as we close this study, I want you to remember who you are. YOU are a daughter of The King! You are chosen, dearly loved, gifted, and so much more. Just as God has called your husband into law enforcement, YOU are also called, and the Lord has equipped you with everything you need to accomplish your tasks well.

Take a moment to reflect on all we've talked about over the last several weeks. Write out a prayer to God asking Him to help you in the areas you struggle with, and thank Him for the areas you excel. I promise, sweet one, He is with you holding your hands tightly around that rope!!

Dear Father...

Until next time,

Kristi

TO SCHEDULE

Kristi Neace

FOR YOUR NEXT EVENT, CONTACT:

Badge of Hope Ministries
P.O. Box 113
Union, MO 63084

badgeofhope2014@gmail.com

neacekr@yahoo.com

www.badgeofhopeministries.com

www.kristineace.com

Also by *Kristi...*

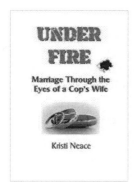

ISBN-10: 1512190578

ISBN-10: 1453677836

ISBN-10: 1461025656

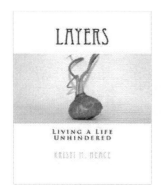

ISBN-10: 1480146218

ISBN-10: 1494295679

ISBN-10: 1490924892

A Letter from Kristi

Dear Friend,

If you're reading this letter, then it means you've probably completed this study, or are perhaps simply thumbing through.

I want you to know that I wrote this study with you in mind, because I understand what it's like to be married to the badge. I, also, wanted to somehow encourage you in your walk with the Lord.

No marriage will ever be great, no personal journey ever completely fulfilling until and unless you give your heart to God and allow Him to take you on the greatest ride of your life.

I don't know where you are in your spiritual journey. I have no idea if you've walked an aisle, been baptized, sprinkled, born again, or whatever you may call it. Perhaps you've not been to church since you were little, or maybe never.

You might be thinking, "I'm not good enough," or "I don't know anything about the Bible," or "We just can't seem to make it there on Sunday mornings".

Let me just tell you something…God came down from heaven in the person of His Son, Jesus, and walked among men and women teaching them the truths of the Bible and loving on them when no-one else would. Jesus walked with the outcasts, ate with sinners, healed the sick and raised the dead.

He did not choose to only love the perfect or the sinless, but gave His life on the cross for *all* so that whomever would believe: He is the Son of God, that He died on the cross for our sins, and rose back to life on the third day, would experience new life and an eternity spent with Him in heaven.

Today, if you do not have a personal relationship with Jesus, stop what you're doing and pray to Him right now. Tell Him that you know you're a sinner (someone who has broken God's laws), that you believe He died for you on the cross, and that you want Him to be Lord of your life and forgive you of your sins. It's that easy!

I hope you have been encouraged today. Stay the course, sweet friend. God loves you, sees you, and will help you through.

Blessings,

Kristi

62436197R00046

Made in the USA
Lexington, KY
07 April 2017